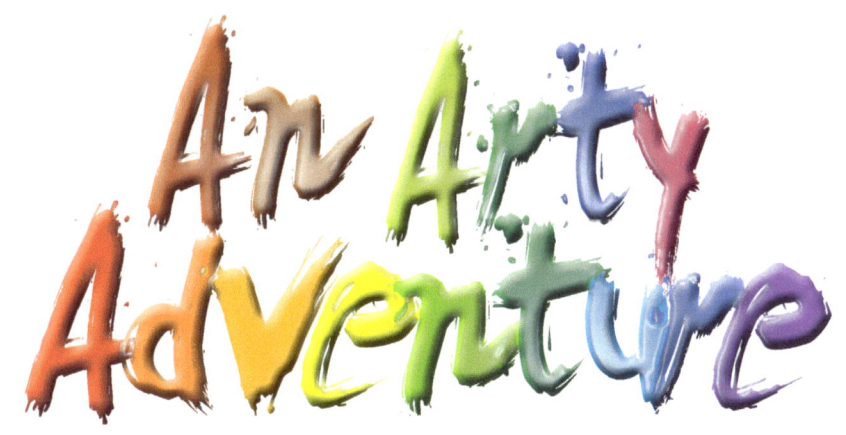

An Arty Adventure

A Young Girl's Journey Toward Abstraction

Sherry Linger Kaier

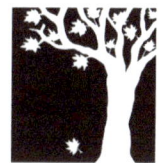

The Artists' Orchard, LLC

REFERENCES

De la Croix, Horst and Tansey, Richard G. ART THROUGH THE AGES, Eighth Edition. New York: Harcourt Brace Jovanovich, Publishers, 1986.

Gruitrooy, Gerhard. VAN GOGH, AN APPRECIATION OF HIS ART. New York: Smithmark Publishers, Inc., 1994.

Hunter, Sam and Jacobus, John. Modern Art, Third Edition. Englewood Cliffs, NJ: Prentice Hall, Inc., 1992 and New York: Harry N. Abrams, Inc., 1992.

Koja, Stephan. Gustav Klimt, LANDSCAPES. Munich: Prestel, 2002, Plate 39.

CONTRIBUTING ARTISTS

Alec Kaier, age 4, drew STAR on page 4.

Gilian Kaier, age 6, drew TURTLE on page 5.

Text and Illustrations copyright © 2010 Sherry Linger Kaier

ISBN: 978-0-9843166-2-5

Library of Congress Control Number: 2010910140

The Artists' Orchard, LLC
P.O. Box 113317
Pittsburgh, PA 15241
www.theartistsorchard.com

Printed in the United States of America

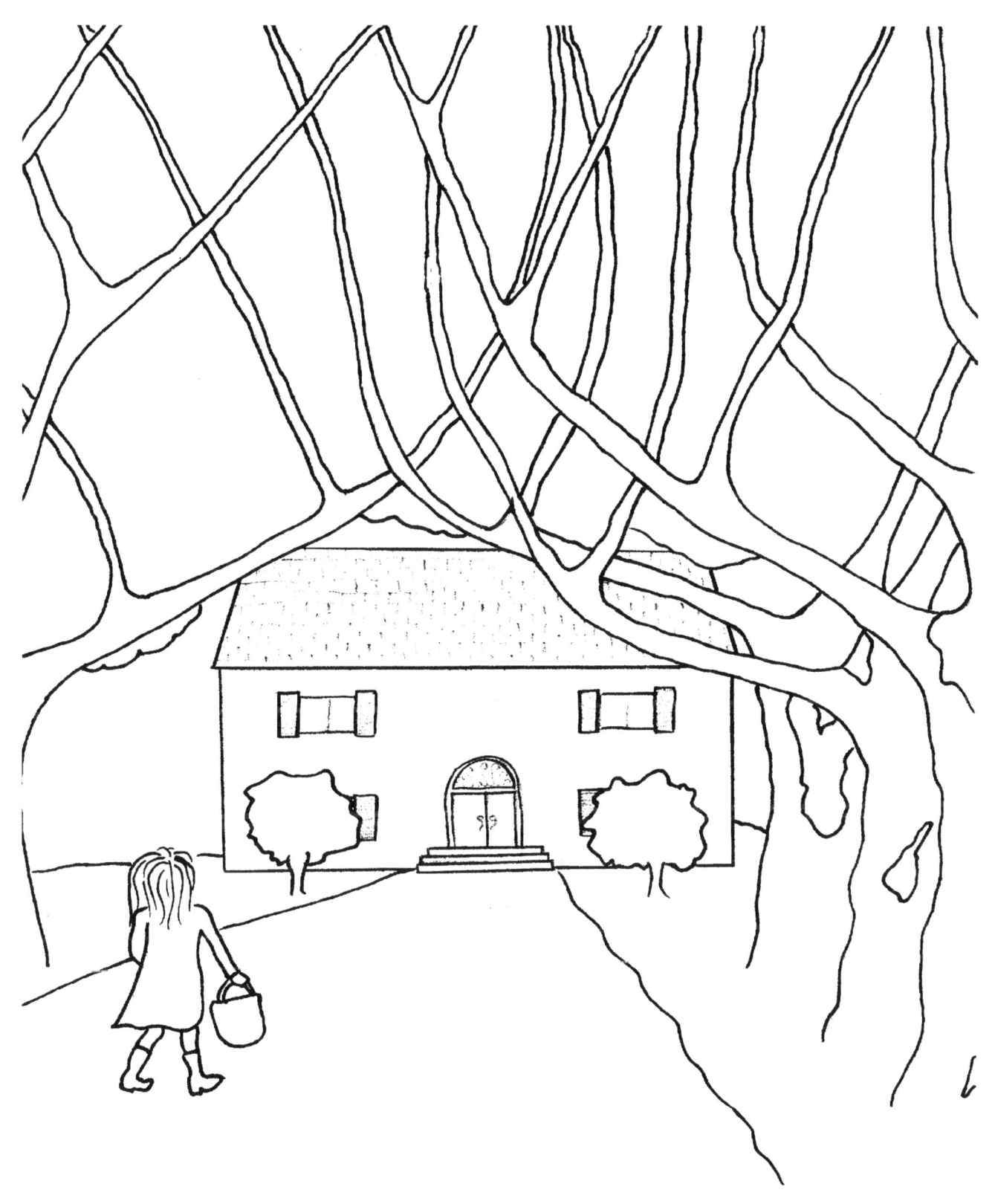

for aspiring artists of all ages

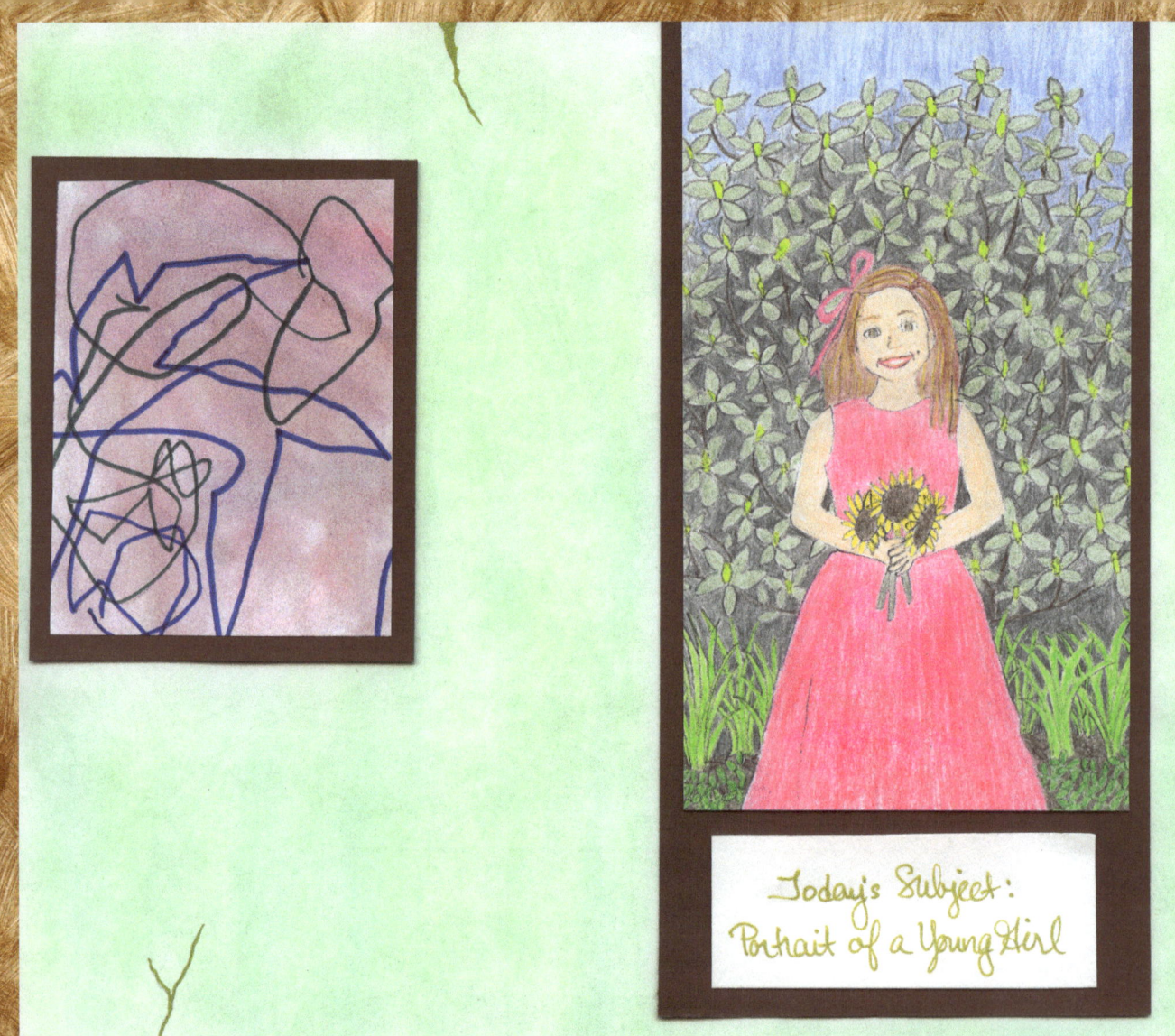

Today's Subject:
Portrait of a Young Girl

My love-hate relationship with art began in this classroom. This is where I fell in love with art - the colors, the strokes and the uniqueness of so many masterpieces. Amazed by the beauty and intrigued by the unfamiliar, I was swept off my feet. Yes, my love of art was strong. However, when asked to imitate those same qualities that I loved, I only felt frustrated. No matter how hard I tried, I couldn't get my projects to look exactly like the original. That was what I hated about my relationship with art.

When I heard the next assignment, I was instantly upset . . . I felt sick with worry. Our teacher wanted us to look at the drawing "Portrait of a Young Girl" and recreate that same image in our own style. So my mental rambling began. If I can't even copy other artists, then how am I supposed to create my own style? I mean I'm just Ava Noodlenicker, not some famous artist! Seriously, how can the teacher expect me to do this?

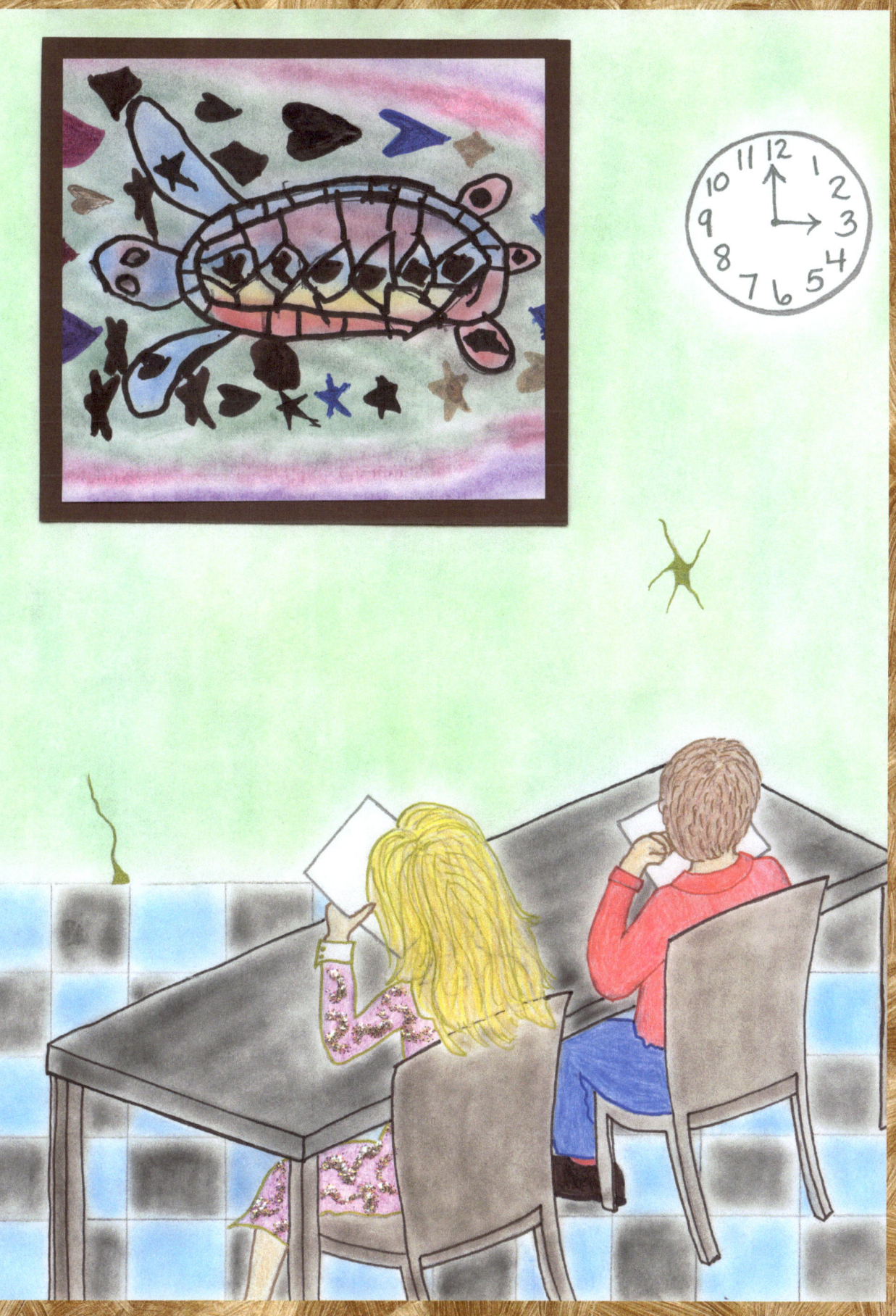

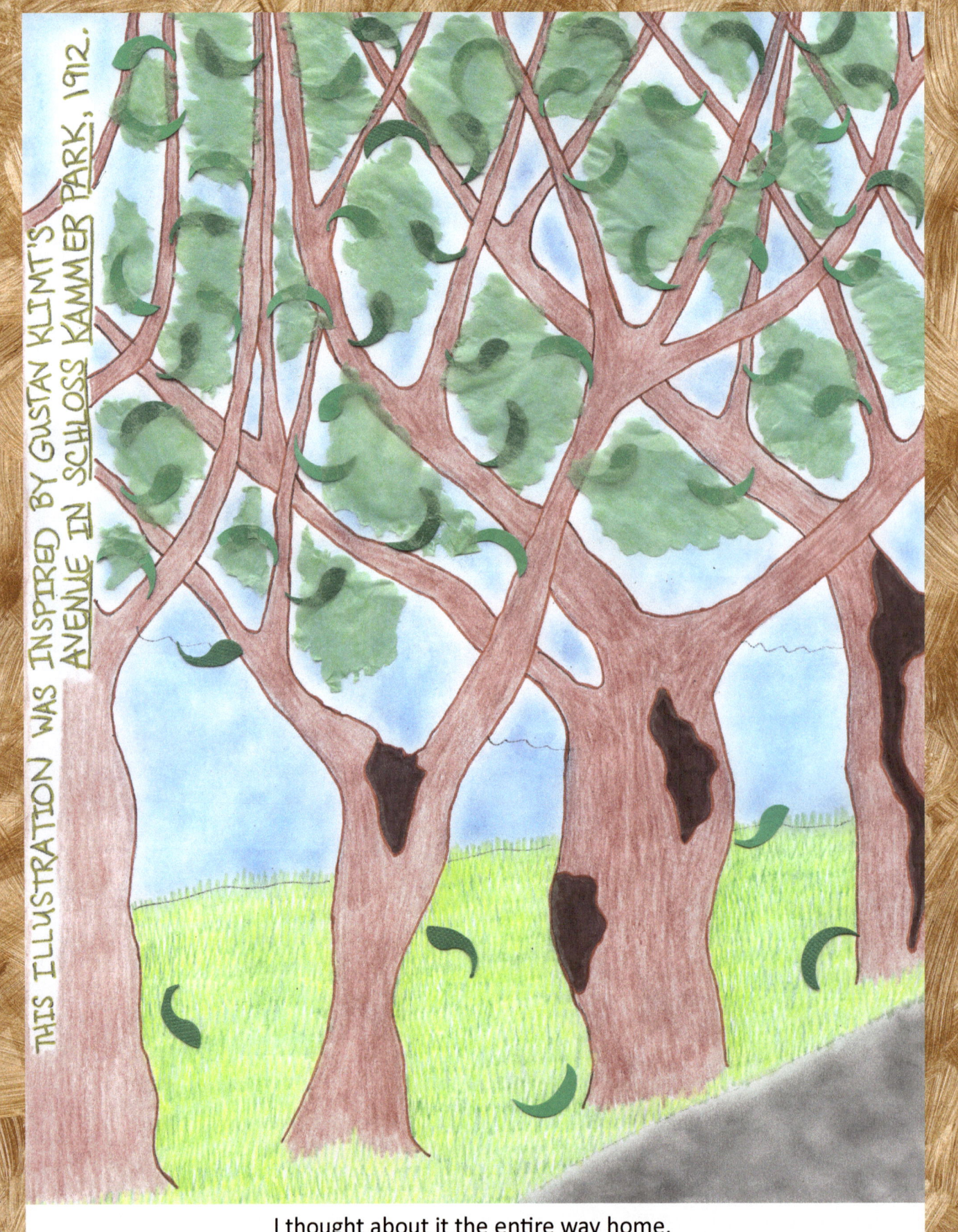

THIS ILLUSTRATION WAS INSPIRED BY GUSTAV KLIMT'S AVENUE IN SCHLOSS KAMMER PARK, 1912.

I thought about it the entire way home.

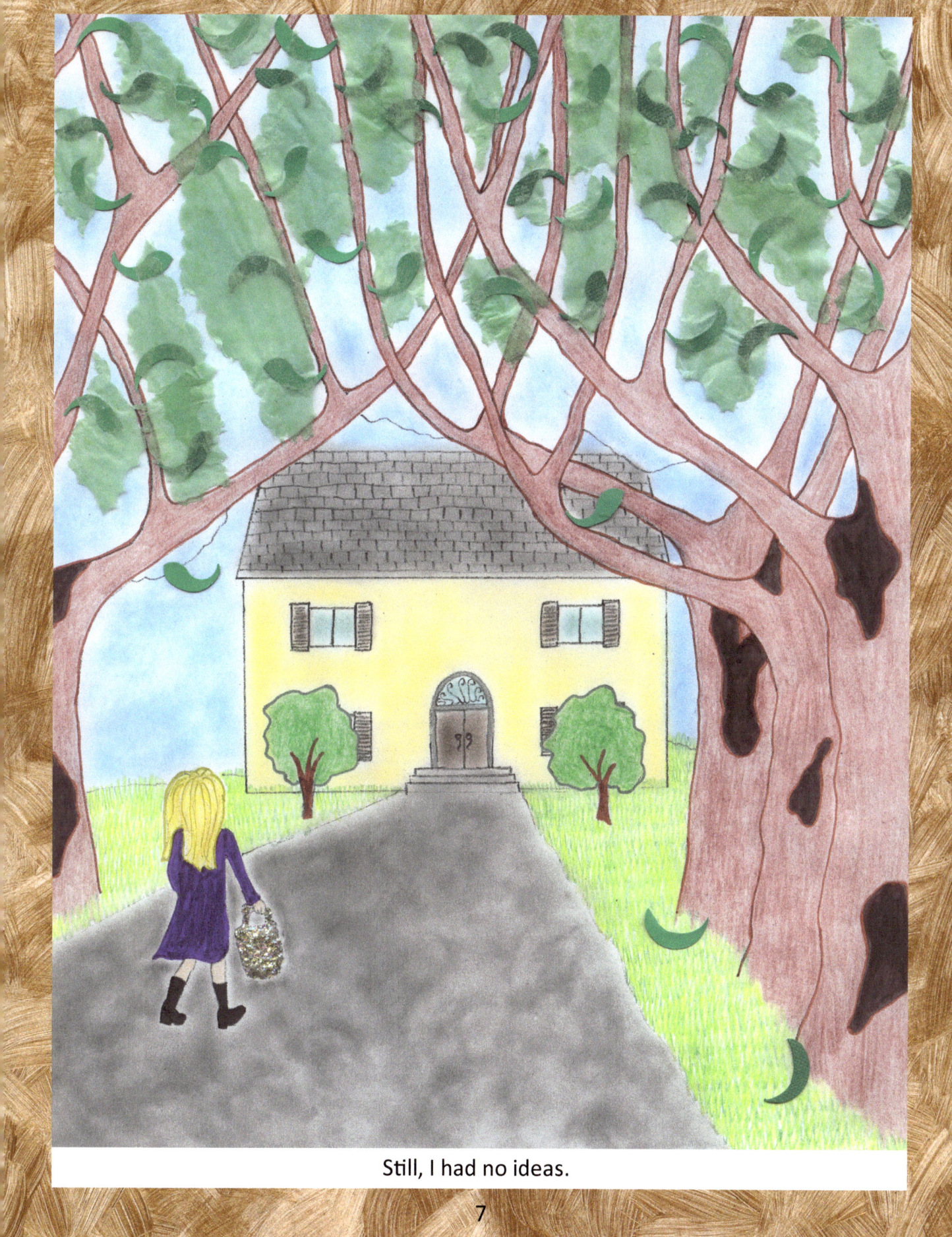

Still, I had no ideas.

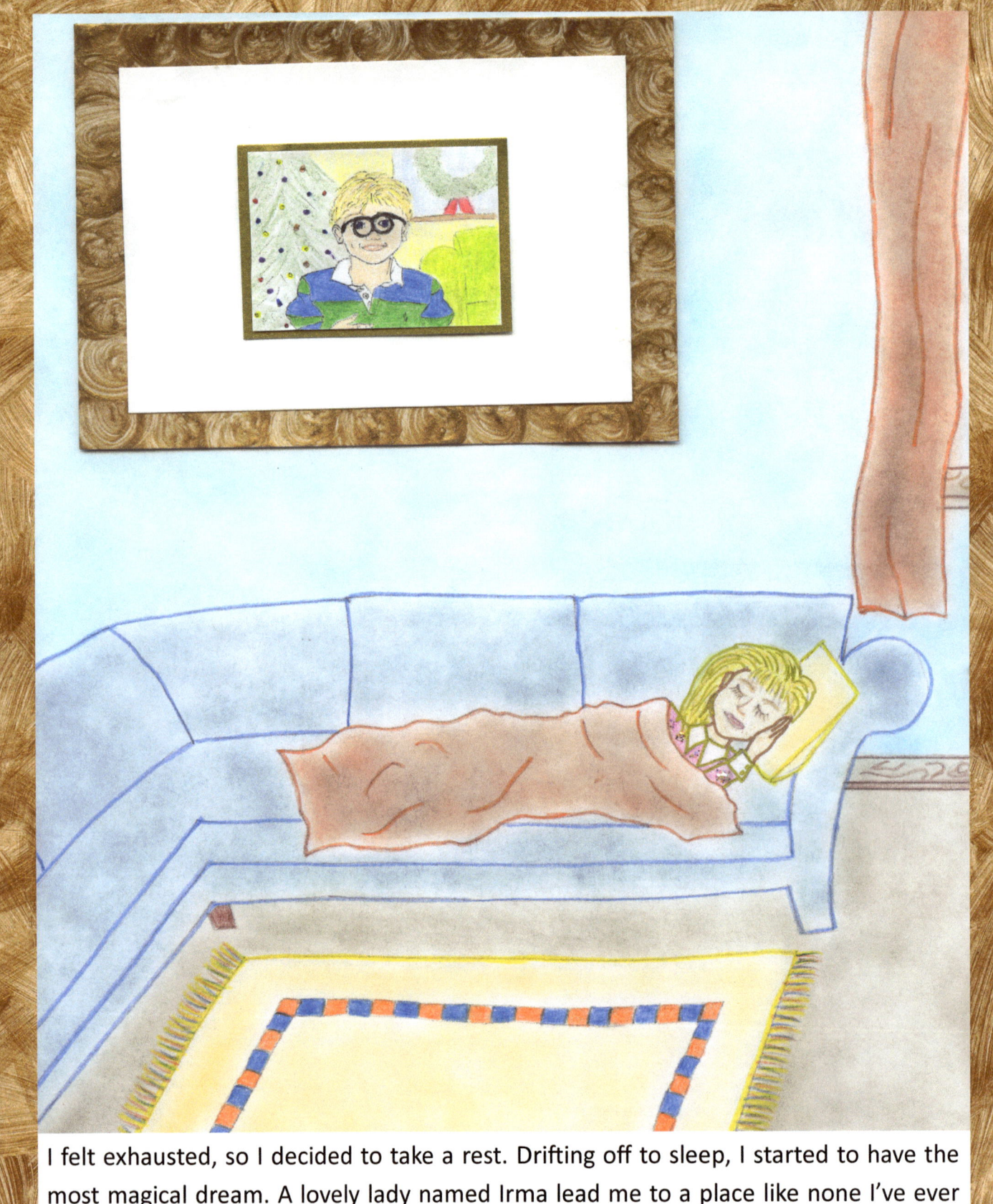

I felt exhausted, so I decided to take a rest. Drifting off to sleep, I started to have the most magical dream. A lovely lady named Irma lead me to a place like none I've ever seen, a place where art grows on trees and is clearly explained. Would you like to see it with me?

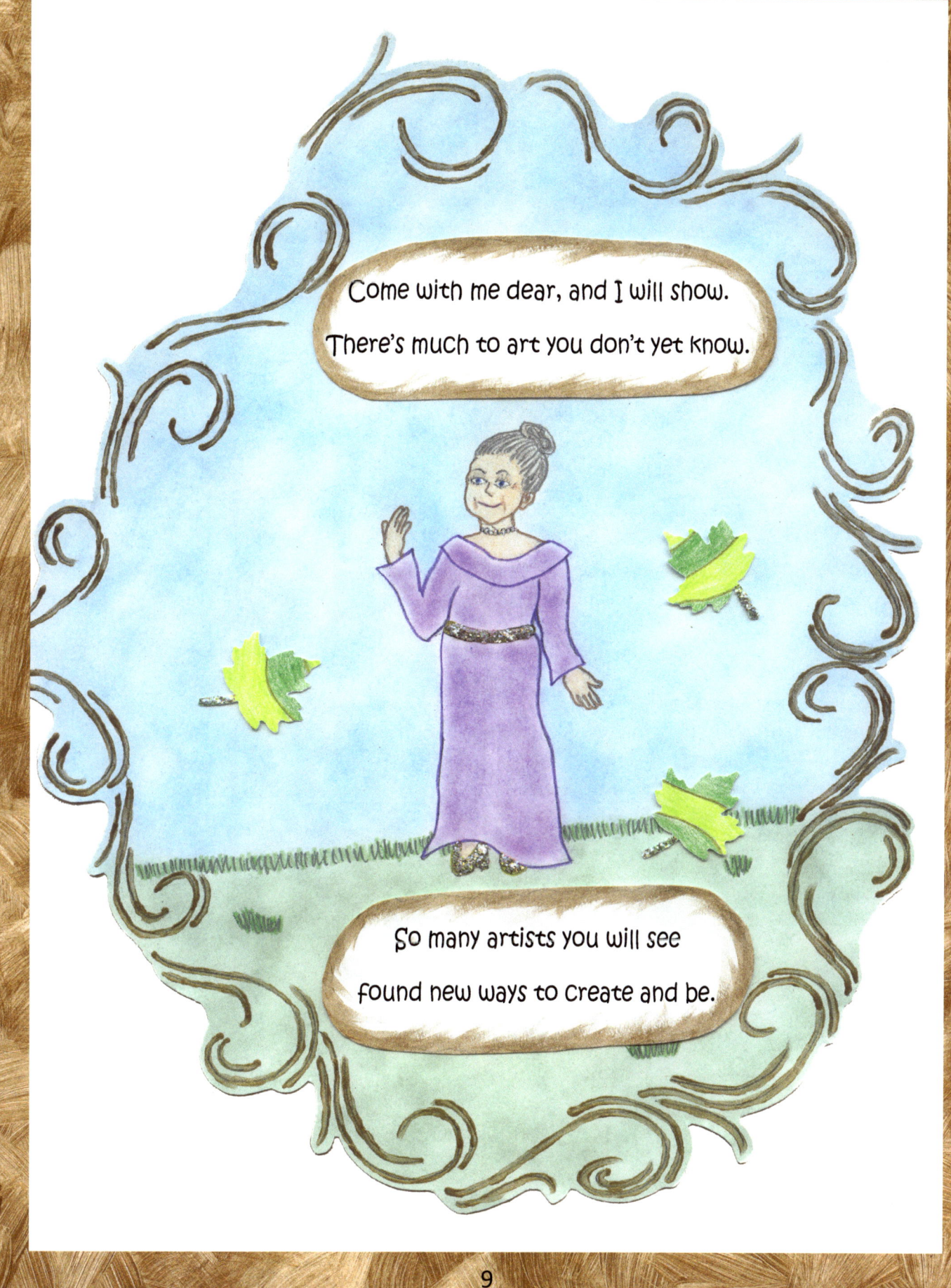

Come with me dear, and I will show.

There's much to art you don't yet know.

So many artists you will see

found new ways to create and be.

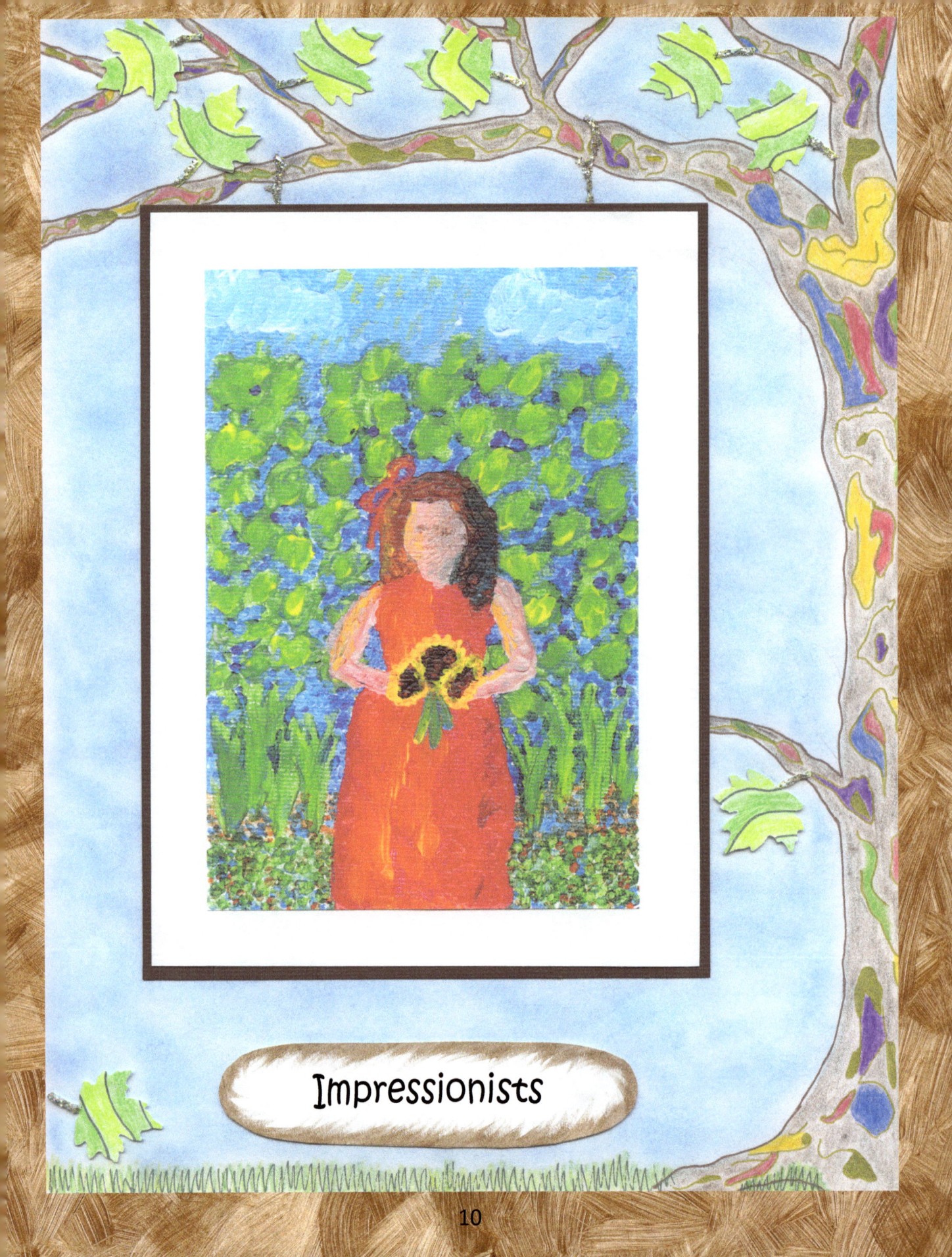

Impressionists

Observing shades from dawn 'til night

Impressionists paint spots of light.

Impressionists paint what colors they see depending on how the sun is shining on an object. They make many paintings of the same thing, a series, to show that an object's colors look different at different times of the day. For instance, the leaves on the rhododendron below have more yellow in the afternoon sun (on the left) and more blue in the morning sun (on the right).

Since Impressionist painters prefer to paint outside, en plein air, instead of in a studio, they have to finish each painting before the lighting changes. Completing paintings so quickly does not leave time to paint small details or to carefully mix the paints before placing them on the canvas. In this painting of the young girl, we do not see small details or any shapes defined by lines. But, do you see the yellow patches where the sunlight hits? Do you notice the many colors that show us rough shapes of the girl and the leaves?

My favorite Impressionist is Auguste Renoir. Who is yours?

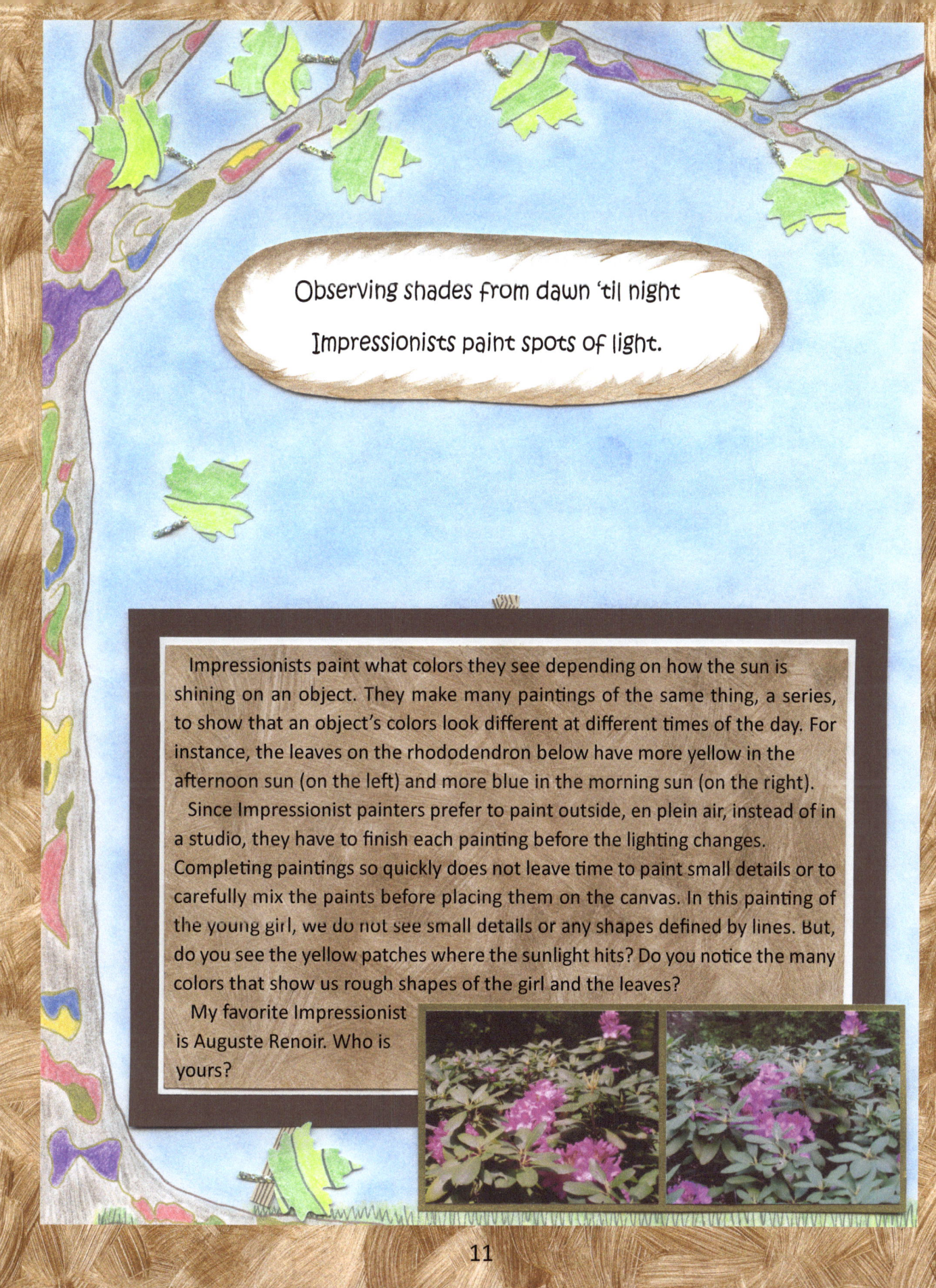

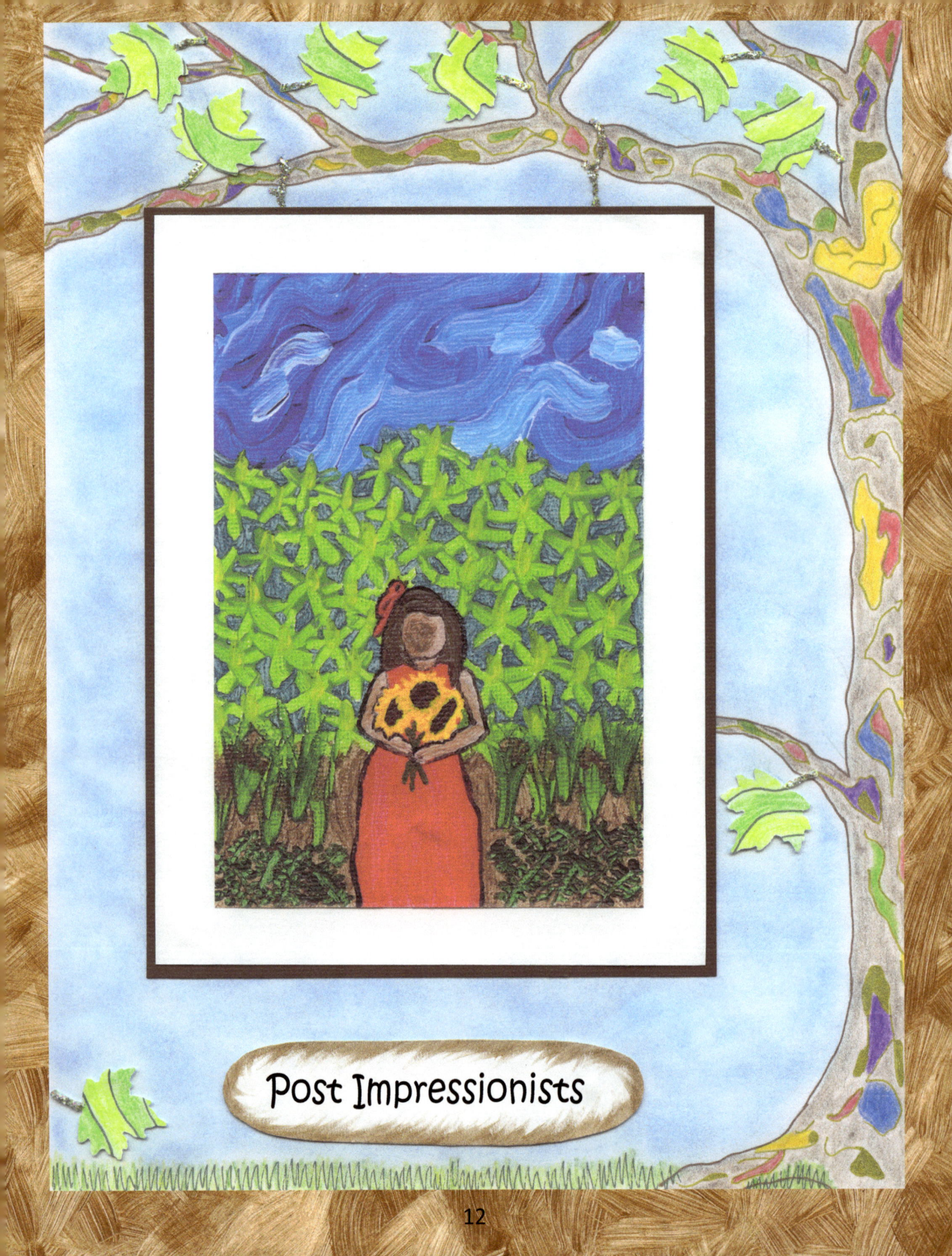

Post Impressionists

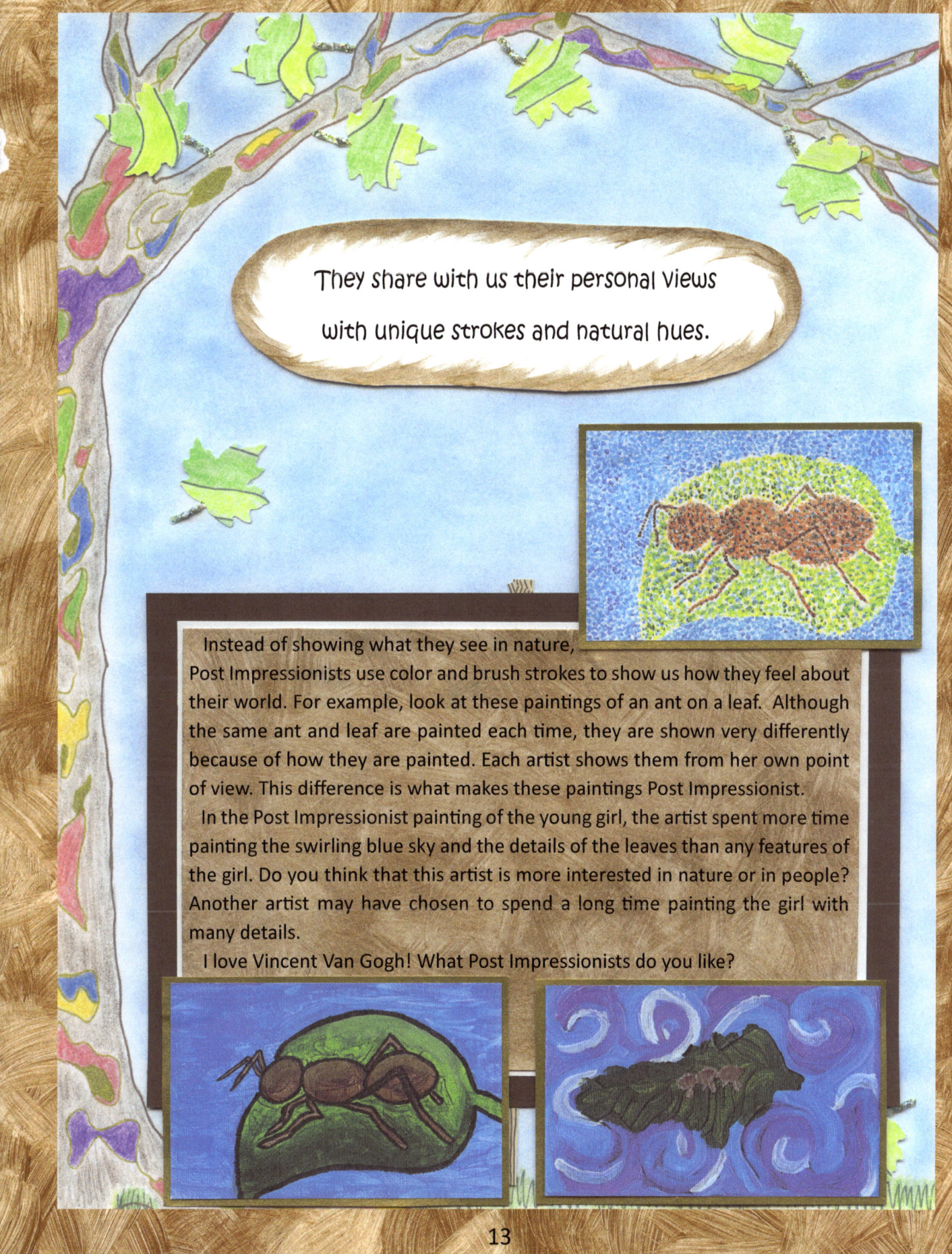

They share with us their personal views
with unique strokes and natural hues.

Instead of showing what they see in nature, Post Impressionists use color and brush strokes to show us how they feel about their world. For example, look at these paintings of an ant on a leaf. Although the same ant and leaf are painted each time, they are shown very differently because of how they are painted. Each artist shows them from her own point of view. This difference is what makes these paintings Post Impressionist.

In the Post Impressionist painting of the young girl, the artist spent more time painting the swirling blue sky and the details of the leaves than any features of the girl. Do you think that this artist is more interested in nature or in people? Another artist may have chosen to spend a long time painting the girl with many details.

I love Vincent Van Gogh! What Post Impressionists do you like?

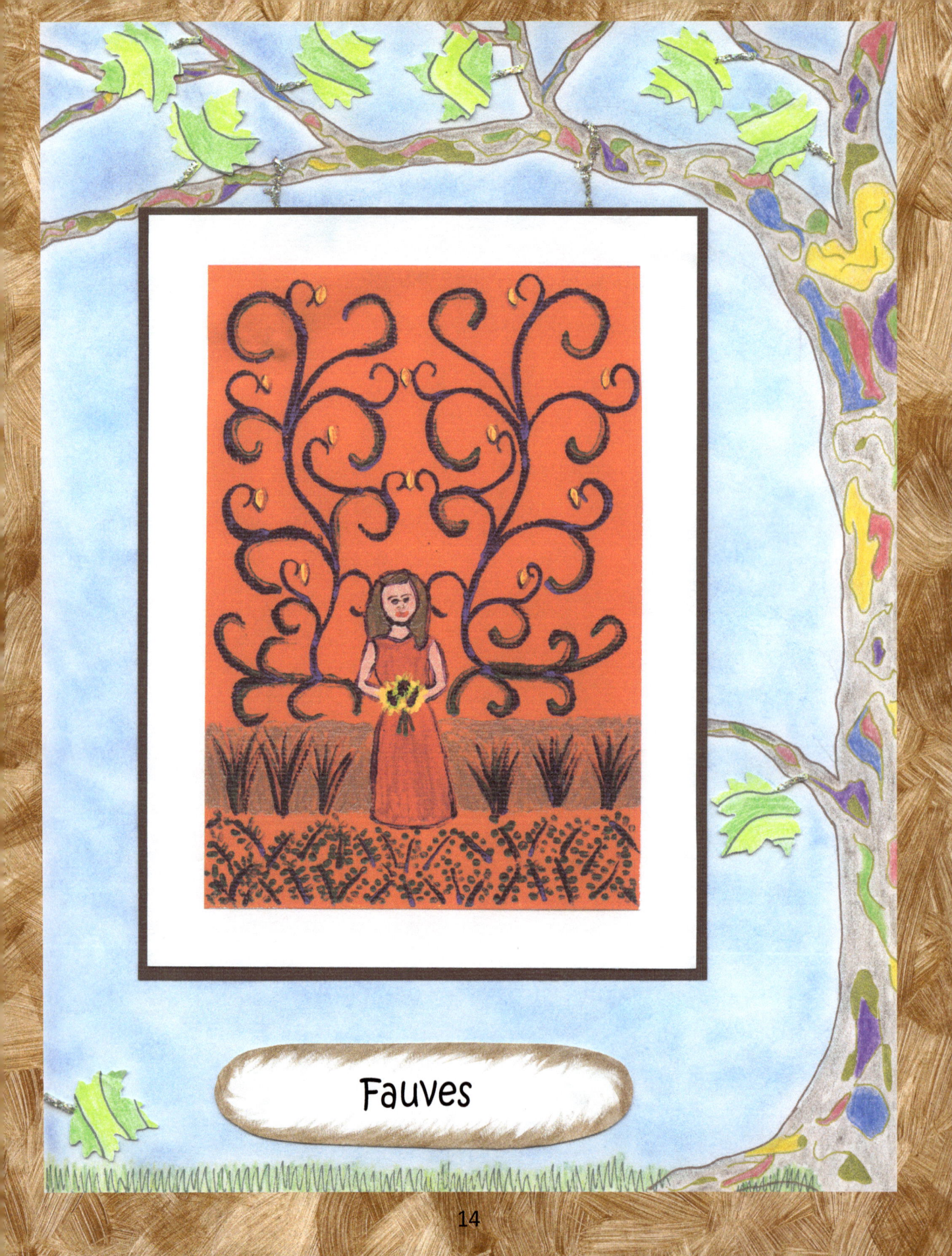

Fauves

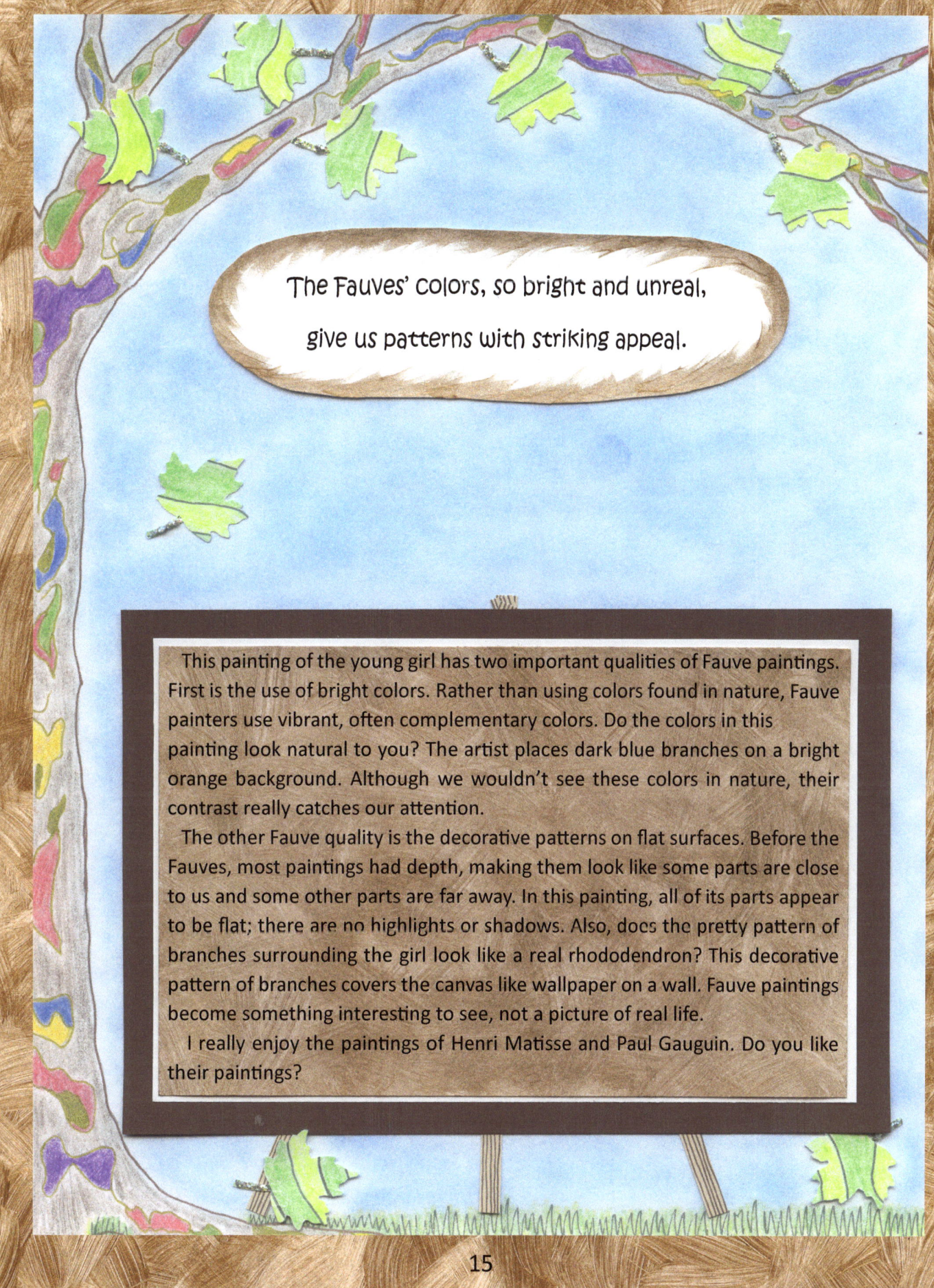

The Fauves' colors, so bright and unreal,

give us patterns with striking appeal.

This painting of the young girl has two important qualities of Fauve paintings. First is the use of bright colors. Rather than using colors found in nature, Fauve painters use vibrant, often complementary colors. Do the colors in this painting look natural to you? The artist places dark blue branches on a bright orange background. Although we wouldn't see these colors in nature, their contrast really catches our attention.

The other Fauve quality is the decorative patterns on flat surfaces. Before the Fauves, most paintings had depth, making them look like some parts are close to us and some other parts are far away. In this painting, all of its parts appear to be flat; there are no highlights or shadows. Also, does the pretty pattern of branches surrounding the girl look like a real rhododendron? This decorative pattern of branches covers the canvas like wallpaper on a wall. Fauve paintings become something interesting to see, not a picture of real life.

I really enjoy the paintings of Henri Matisse and Paul Gauguin. Do you like their paintings?

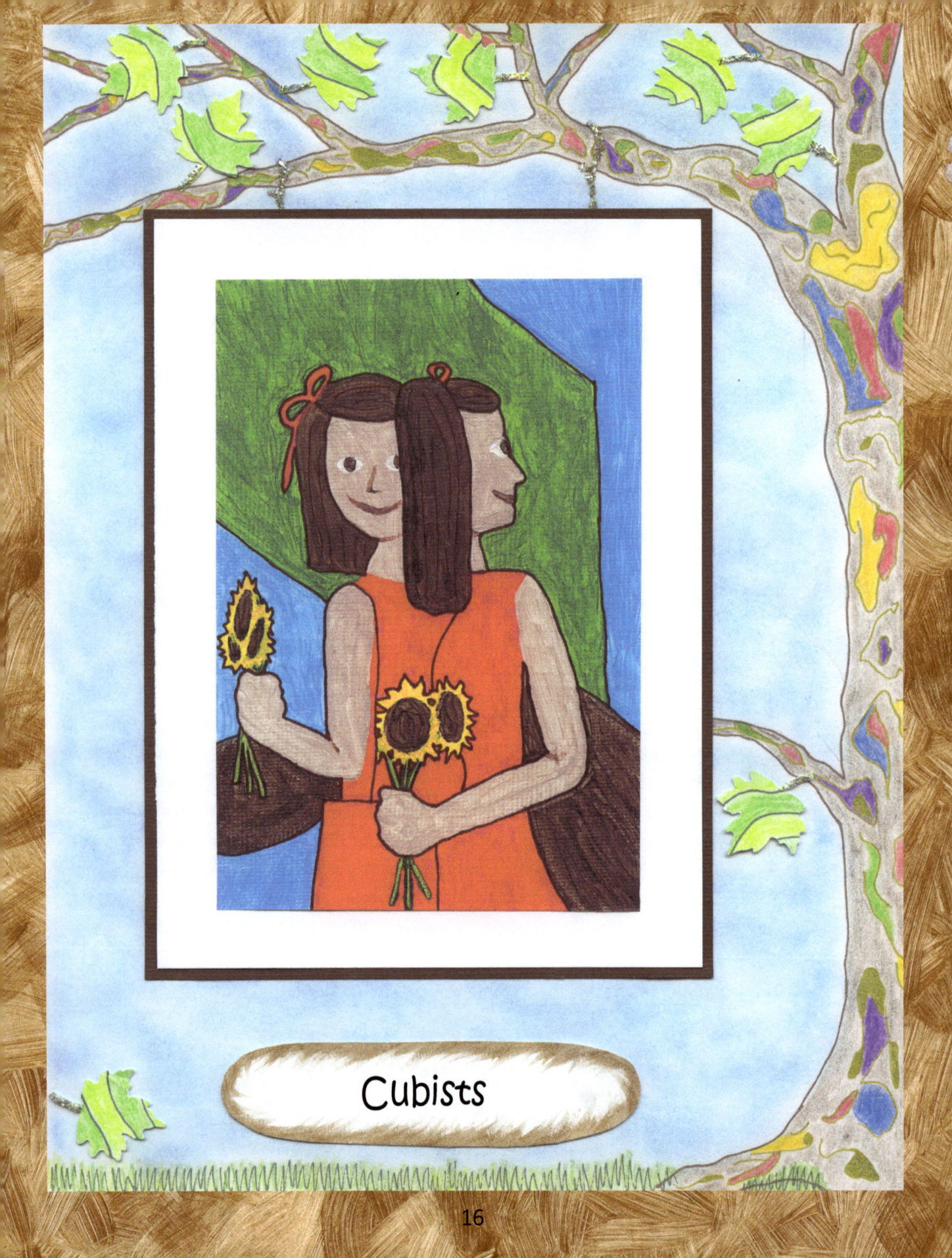

Cubists

The Cubists paint so many views showing objects as if they move.

   Most paintings show objects from one view like we see them with our own eyes. Cubist paintings show several different views of the same object all on one canvas. Since we do not usually see many views of an object at the same time, Cubism may seem difficult to understand. Really, Cubist painters just show us things in a new way.

   Imagine that the girl in the painting spins around slowly. Your view of her would change with each turn that she makes. As she turns, you would see her side, then her back, then her other side, and finally, the front of her again. Instead of showing each of the views on a new canvas, the artist paints several views on just one canvas. So in this painting, we see the front, the back and the side of her head and, separately, we see the front, the back and the side of her body all at the same time. Do you see it?

   I think that Pablo Picasso was a true trailblazer with his Cubist paintings. Do you like any of his paintings?

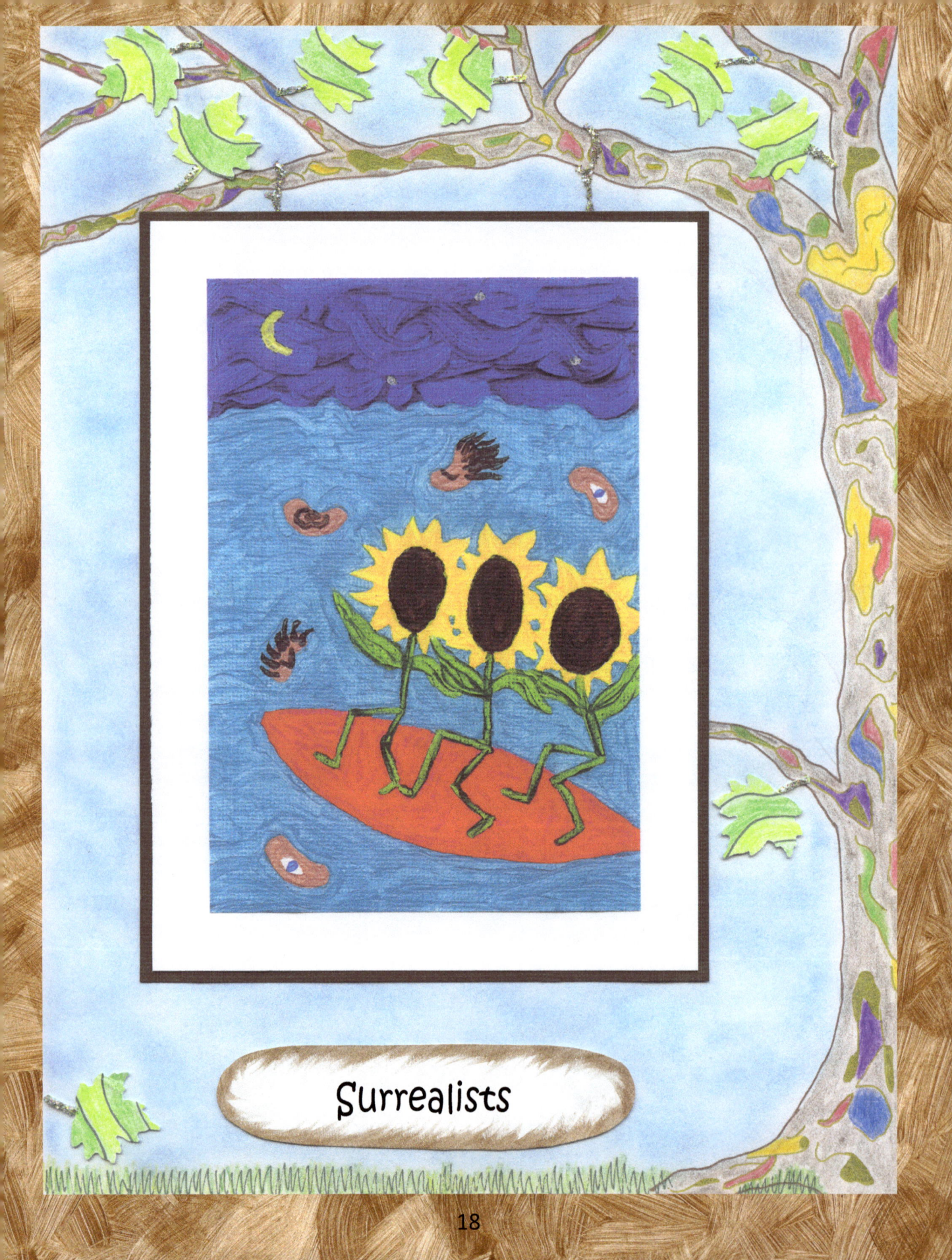

Surrealists

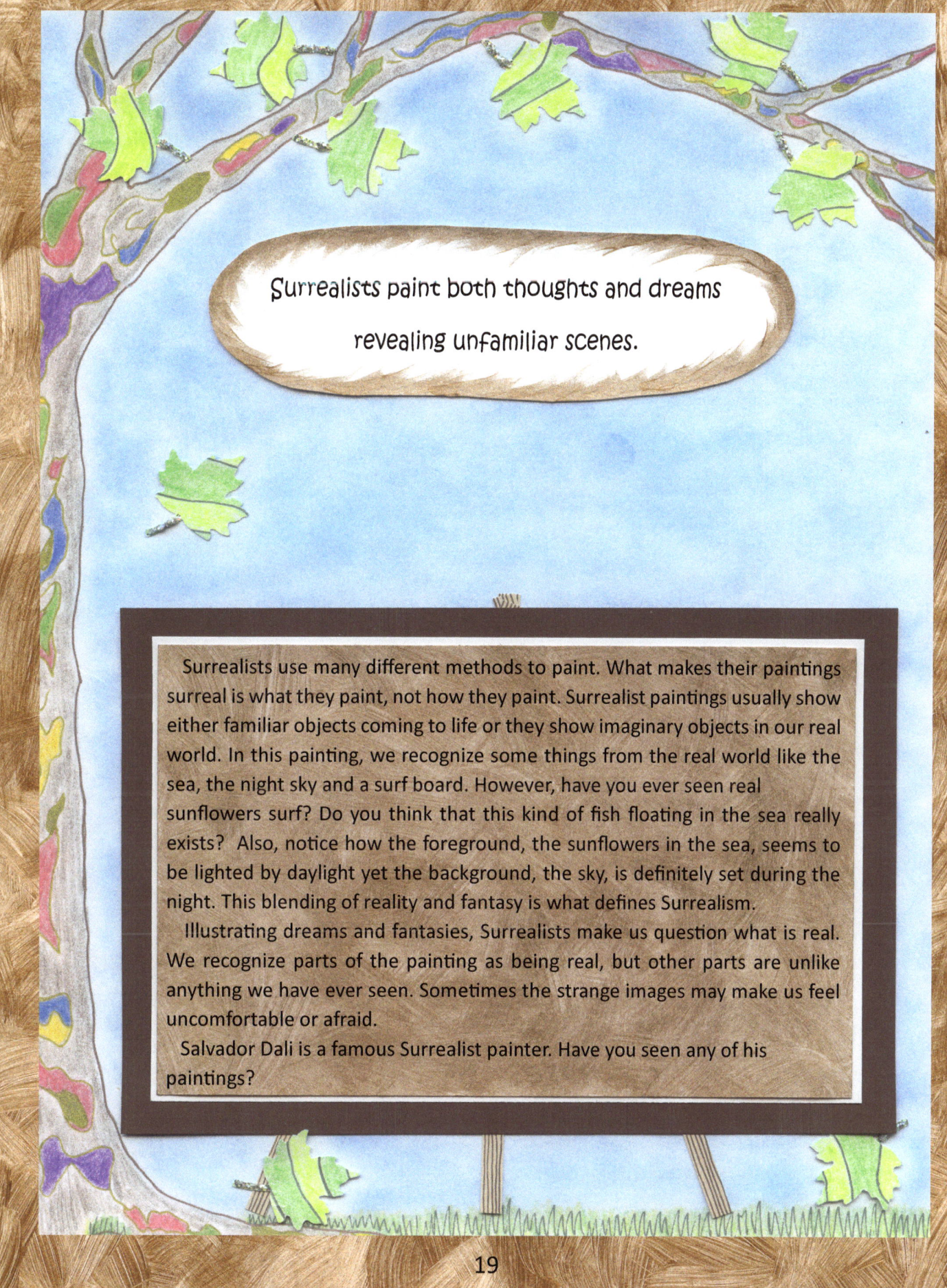

Surrealists paint both thoughts and dreams revealing unfamiliar scenes.

Surrealists use many different methods to paint. What makes their paintings surreal is what they paint, not how they paint. Surrealist paintings usually show either familiar objects coming to life or they show imaginary objects in our real world. In this painting, we recognize some things from the real world like the sea, the night sky and a surf board. However, have you ever seen real sunflowers surf? Do you think that this kind of fish floating in the sea really exists? Also, notice how the foreground, the sunflowers in the sea, seems to be lighted by daylight yet the background, the sky, is definitely set during the night. This blending of reality and fantasy is what defines Surrealism.

Illustrating dreams and fantasies, Surrealists make us question what is real. We recognize parts of the painting as being real, but other parts are unlike anything we have ever seen. Sometimes the strange images may make us feel uncomfortable or afraid.

Salvador Dali is a famous Surrealist painter. Have you seen any of his paintings?

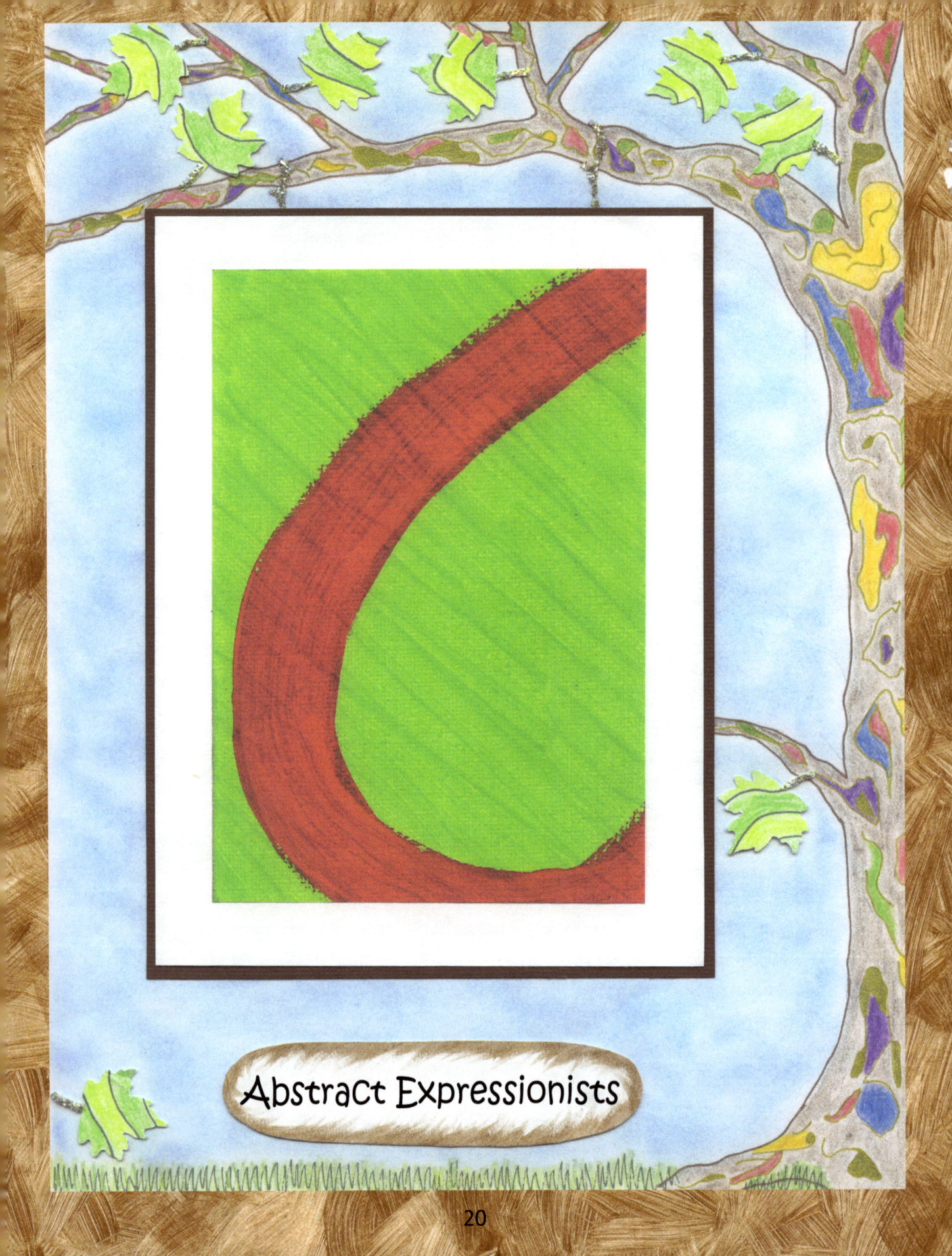

Abstract Expressionists

The paints flow so free and abstract
showing us the painterly act.

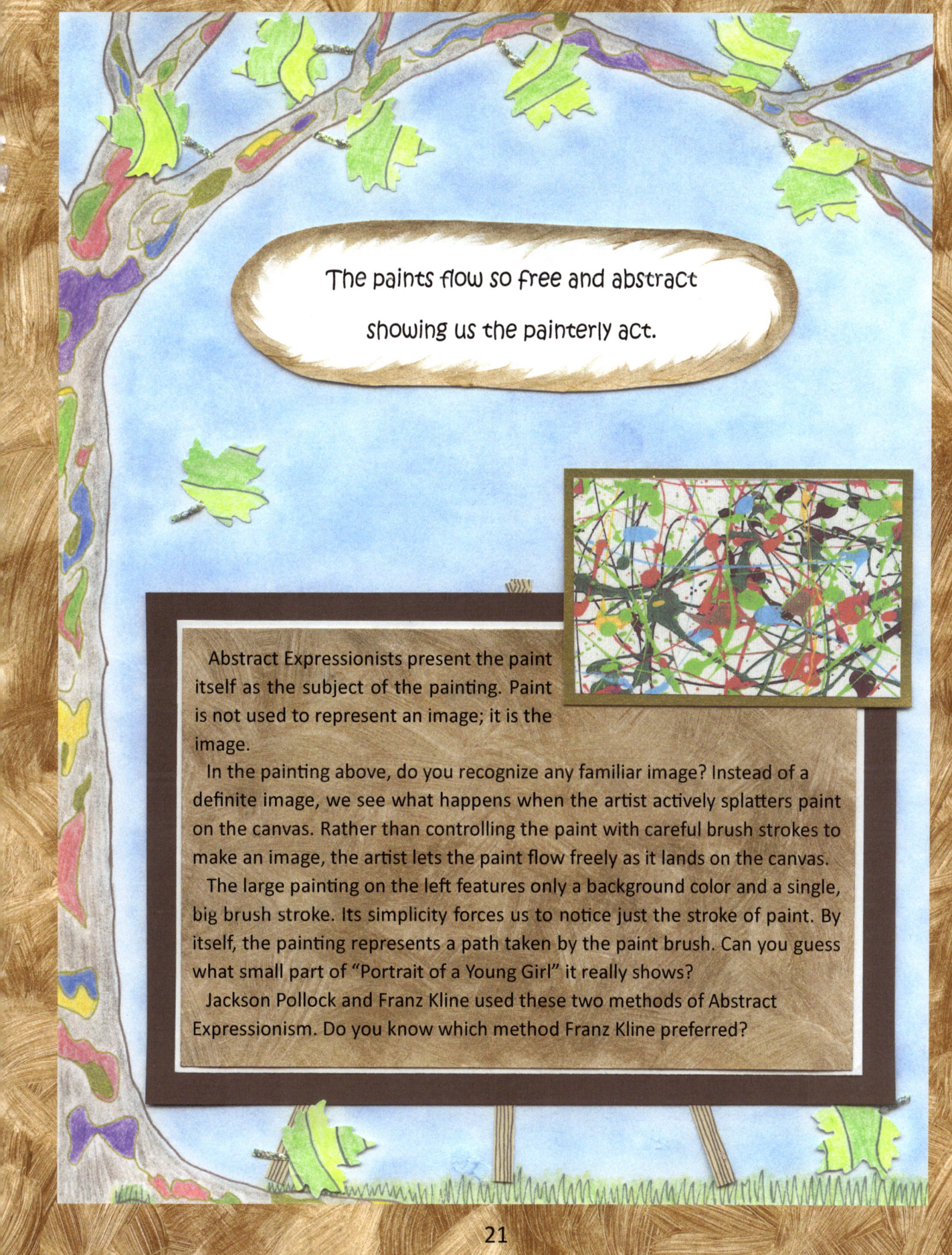

Abstract Expressionists present the paint itself as the subject of the painting. Paint is not used to represent an image; it is the image.

In the painting above, do you recognize any familiar image? Instead of a definite image, we see what happens when the artist actively splatters paint on the canvas. Rather than controlling the paint with careful brush strokes to make an image, the artist lets the paint flow freely as it lands on the canvas.

The large painting on the left features only a background color and a single, big brush stroke. Its simplicity forces us to notice just the stroke of paint. By itself, the painting represents a path taken by the paint brush. Can you guess what small part of "Portrait of a Young Girl" it really shows?

Jackson Pollock and Franz Kline used these two methods of Abstract Expressionism. Do you know which method Franz Kline preferred?

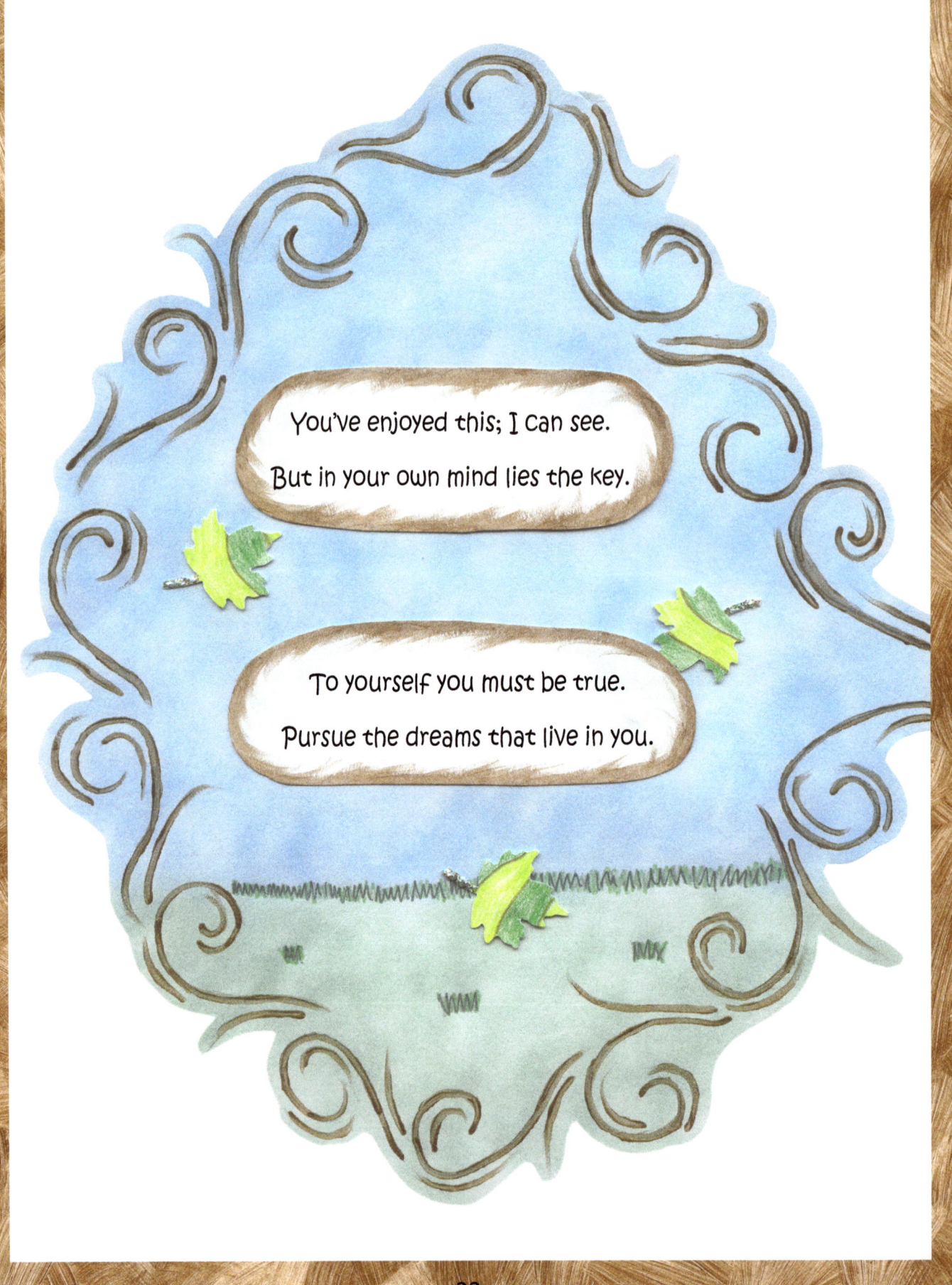

You've enjoyed this; I can see.

But in your own mind lies the key.

To yourself you must be true.

Pursue the dreams that live in you.

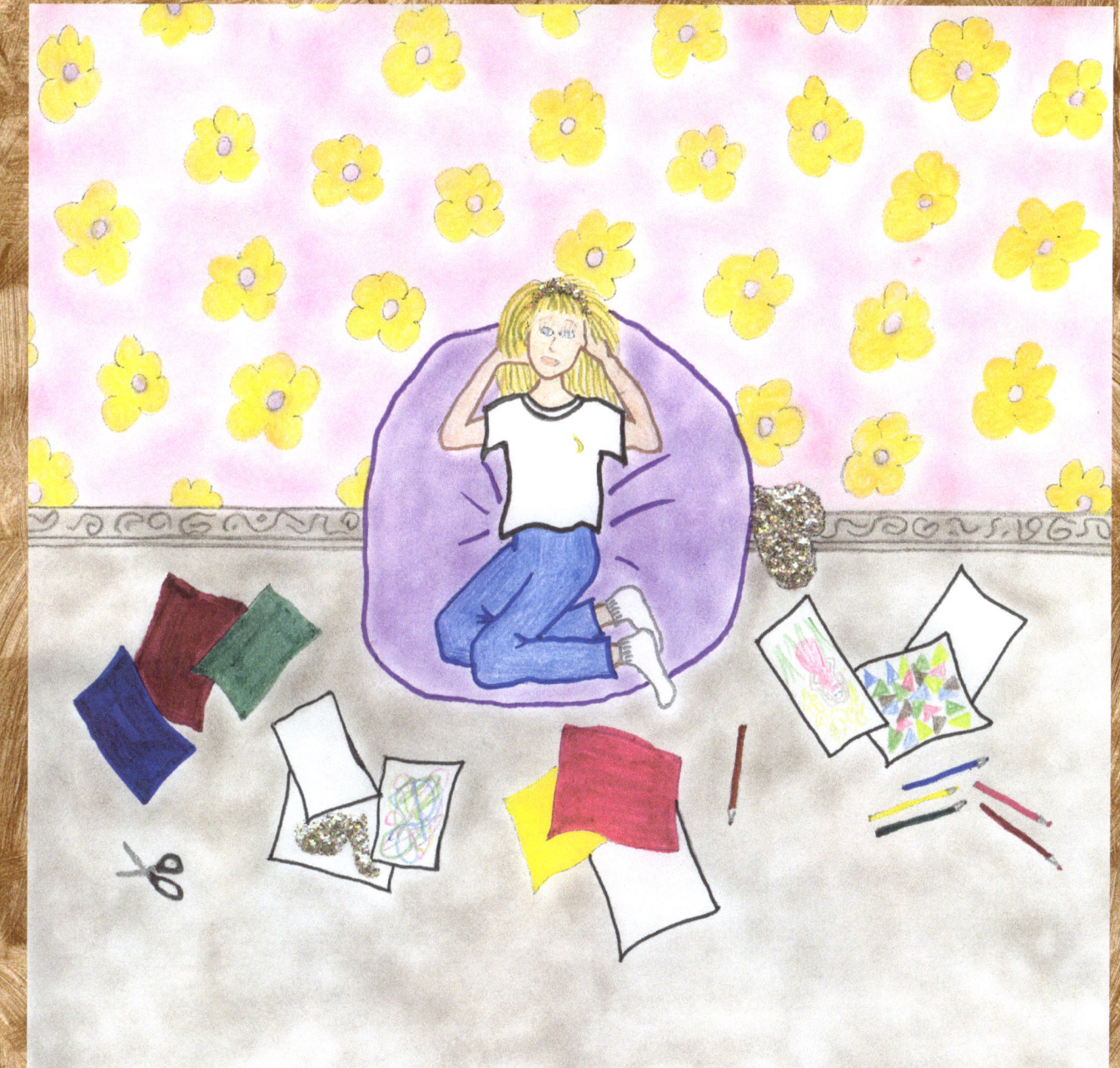

Wow! Wasn't that amazing? I learned so much from Irma. She explained how different the art movements are, but I think I discovered what they all have in common, too. All of the artists chose to represent their subject in their own personal ways. They didn't try to make their art like anyone else's. That originality is what makes a great artist.

That gave me an idea. Maybe I had been approaching my new assignment all wrong. Instead of looking at other people's art for inspiration I should have been thinking about how I feel and what I like.

After thinking about projects that I have enjoyed, I began experimenting. I used every art supply I could find and tried every method I knew. Then it came to me.

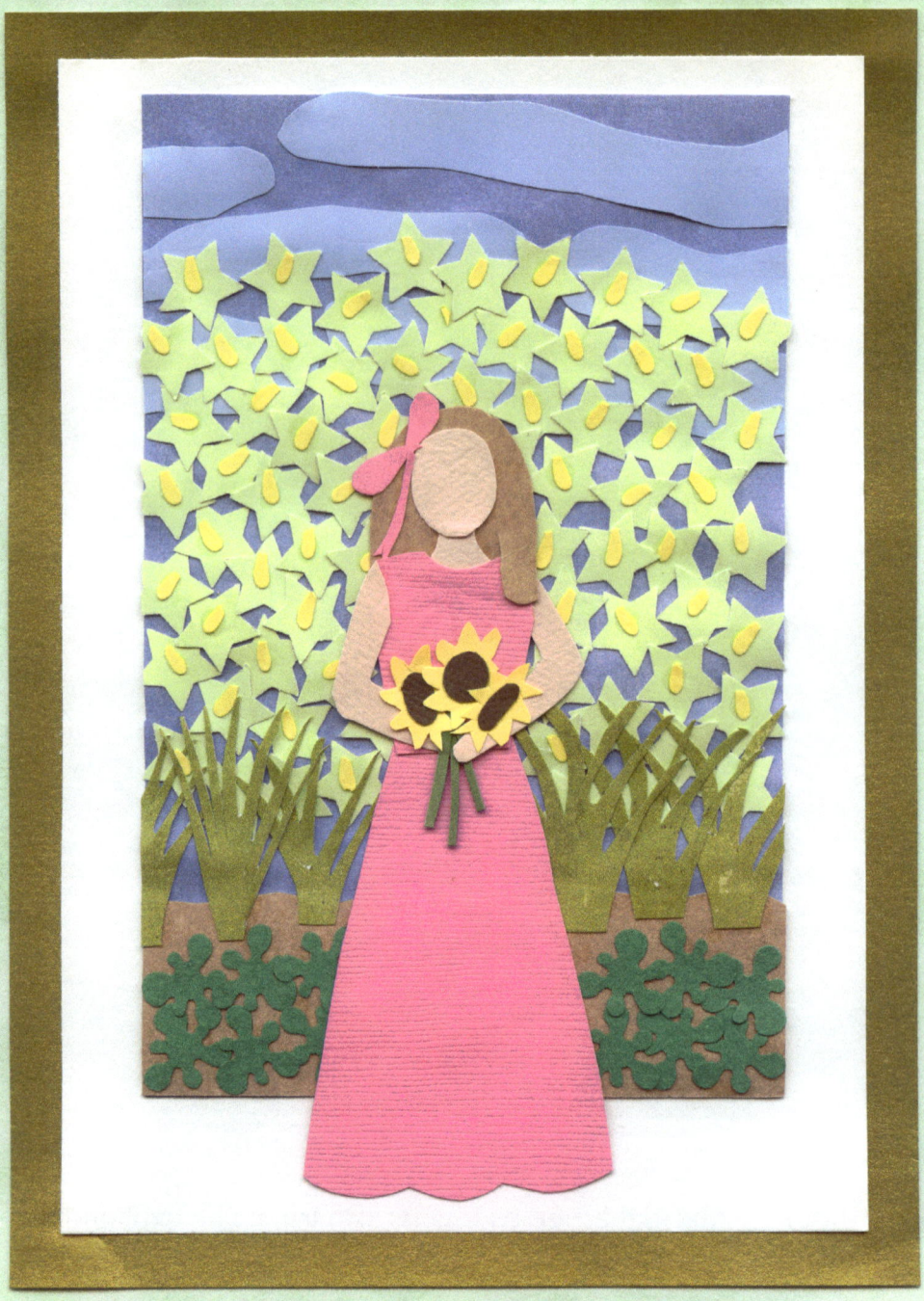

Since life can be so confusing, I wanted my art to be simple. I used paper cut-outs to show clearly defined shapes and colors, and I presented the young girl as the most significant part.

Both my friends and my teacher were impressed with my artwork. It did turn out pretty well, if I do say so myself. Now when I get a new art assignment, I can't wait to get started!

From the Author

Please know that the art movements covered in this book have been simplified so that some basics may be understood by everyone. Art can be very complex. Some people spend their entire lives studying the art of a certain time period, a country, or even a single artist. Lucky for us, we don't have to be so committed. There are plenty of books, museums and internet sites for us to explore.

To see paintings done by some of the original artists whose styles are featured in this book, look up:

IMPRESSIONISTS
Claude Monet, Edgar Degas, Mary Cassatt and Auguste Renoir

POST IMPRESSIONISTS
Vincent Van Gogh, Paul Cezanne and George Seurat

FAUVES
Henri Matisse and Paul Gauguin

CUBISTS
Pablo Picasso and Georges Braques

SURREALISTS
Salvador Dali, Andre Masson and Max Ernst

ABSTRACT EXPRESSIONISTS
Jackson Pollock, Franz Kline and Willem de Kooning

There have been countless talented, interesting artists throughout history. I encourage you to find artists who you like because the rewards are worth the effort. Their art will enrich your life!

Teacher, mom and art lover are all words that describe Sherry Linger Kaier. She has a bachelors degree in Art History from Dickinson College, a Physics teaching certificate, has studied art in Rome and is a proud mom of two. The desire to introduce her children to great art in a fun and creative way is what inspired her to write and illustrate this, her first book.

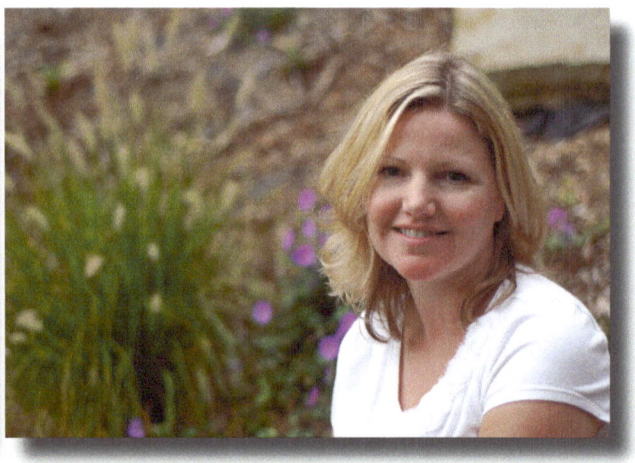